AN ANT'S ADVICE

A FEW PRACTICAL SUGGESTIONS TO TICKLE YOUR HEART AND MIND.

CHIRADEEP PATRA

Made with ♥ on the Notion Press Platform
www.notionpress.com

A writer has no worth without a reader who reads and motivates them to write more. So, I dedicate this book to all my readers, those who love to read and support what I write by weaving the words of my imagination as well as of my life experiences.

I also dedicate this book to those who have inspired me all these years and have prompted me to write such stories.

Above all, I dedicate this book to the One and only Lord God Almighty, my Saviour Jesus Christ, who has been my strength all this time.

Contents

Preface

According to an Animal Kingdom TV Channel documentary, "the Leafcutter Ants can carry more than fifty times their weight only with their jaws," thus ranking them third among the world's strongest creatures. In the book of Proverbs, the Bible speaks of ants as being one of the wisest creatures on the planet, saying, "*Go to the ant, you sluggard; consider its ways and be wise!*"

Ants are considered to be wise because they are not only hardworking but also because they never stop working. We, humans, have been given dominion over all creation. Still, we struggle because of the slackness in our responsibilities - whether in our financial affairs, relationships or workplace issues. That is why we, the sluggards, have been asked to consider learning from the wise ants.

This book is a collection of 15 articles penned from my own experiences, where I initially behaved like a sluggard - in body or mind or spirit - but bounced back in due course of time with the help of wise counsel.

Chiradeep Patra
Author
https://linktr.ee/chiradeep

Acknowledgements

I am so grateful to God for giving me the inspiration and strength to write these articles over the years and now compiling a few as a book to motivate others. Therefore, I humbly acknowledge God, who helped me in my endeavour to reach out to the hearts and minds of my readers.

I am very grateful to ***Christine Mendonza*** for proofreading and editing all these 15 articles that I compiled in this book. She agreed to help me without hesitation despite her responsibilities as a school teacher. I sincerely acknowledge the contribution of her input and suggestions for the improvement of this book.

Savio Paes, my buddy, has always been very supportive throughout these years of my writing. He did the final editing and formatting of the articles. He is the best in the business when it comes to formatting an article. I am thankful to him for extending his helping hands towards this book, from proofreading to editing it wonderfully.

I am indebted to both ***Christine*** and ***Savio*** for their invaluable efforts and contribution in publishing this book.

Ultimately, I thank all my family members and friends far and wide who have always believed in my talent despite being aware of my ill health. Their prayers and steadfast support have made me stand for the Lord and venture ahead to publish this book.

Chiradeep Patra
Author

Acknowledgements

[illegible] and strength to write [illegible] capturing a [illegible] others. *Therefore I humbly acknowledge God, who helped* [illegible] *to reach out to the hearts and minds of my readers.*

I am [illegible] to Christine Mendonca for [illegible] all those [illegible] in this book [illegible] without [illegible] acknowledge [illegible] encouragement of this book.

[illegible]

[illegible] for their invaluable efforts [illegible] this book.

[illegible] have always believed [illegible]

[illegible]

ONE

HONESTY RUNS THROUGH THE BASIC LEVELS OF COURAGE

"Courage is ***the mental or moral strength to venture, persevere, and withstand danger, fear, or difficu***lty"

...according to Merriam-Webster dictionary.

It makes a person stand out in the crowd. It helps a person face the danger or dare of any kind which most doesn't put them into. But along with courage, a person needs mental toughness, physical strength and ability to face that amount of danger or risk and sustain instead of succumbing to the danger easily.

The above is the most generic meaning or higher-level application of the word Courage which only a few selected ones possess. But as per my knowledge and intellect is concerned courage has THREE basic levels of application through which each and every individual on this earth gets an opportunity to go. And I have categorized those THREE levels of courage as under:

*1. **Sincerity** – Do what is right **level of courage:***

With the presence of sin and corruption in our genes we are inclined towards insincerity in our responsibilities often and we do try to justify our degree of insincerity with some reasons like sickness, weakness and so on. So according to me, when we display a sense of courage to do what is right despite our excuses or say and valid reasons, we succeed to earn respect and attention from the people surrounding us.

How many of us are sincere at our workplace all the time? Have we tried to do the extra hours just to finish what was due for us that day? How many times do we procrastinate and keep things pending? Oh, trust me, I am the biggest example of that, sadly. I may blame my ill health. But sincerity is essential to display the minimum level of courage I have to do things that I know to be right and essential.

Sincerity is an attribute which can be displayed at any point of time or place and is not limited to our workplace only. We need to be sincere with our household chores or duties pertaining to our house or families. We need to be sincere even with our friends.

This level of courage that we need is concerning our duties and responsibilities mostly which we display in our actions. But the next level of courage is higher and more challenging.

2. **Honesty** – *Say what is right* **level of courage:**

Dealing with people is more challenging than just doing what is right. We face people at every stage of our life. To say the things which we know to be right and make them follow the same is really difficult. In life, we have some examples of how honesty can put us in danger or at a risk. But the challenge of this level is to have the courage to be honest in our actions as well as what we express.

In the family, while discussing something, I find it extremely difficult to say, "*I don't want to hear anymore, let's discuss it later as I am feeling stressed.*" That was the honest me. But if I say it honestly, then I become selfish, uninterested and escaping. Yeah, it is tough yet we need to be honest.

3. **Justice** – *Stand for what is right* **level of courage:**

This level is tough, as a person must deal with both his or her responsibilities as well as the people around him or her. He or she has to stand for what he or she believes or does or says as right. Doing justice is one thing and protecting the same is all the more difficult and dangerous in a world where everyone tends to do things other than what is right.

For the fear of superiors, when we don't stand for someone who becomes the victim of injustice makes us cowards or have no courage. Standing for justice is deadly and risky. But I believe, if I practice courage at the *sincerity level* and *honesty level* then it will be easier for me to display the courage to be just and protect what is right.

Interestingly, I see the courage of sincerity, honesty and justice working at all levels but honesty is predominant among all. Let me explain as I conclude this article.

In the ***first level*** of courage when we are honest with our self, we become sincere. In the second level, we display the courage of honesty when we are truthful to ourselves as well as with the people, we deal on a day-to-day basis. And at the end, when we are courageous to stand for justice, we are honest to our own selves, honest to the people around us and honest with the creator God who sees everything from above.

Tough? **Really, really tough,** I would say. But there have always been people who have stood out as the ONLY ONE from the mass and have proved that they can do – be sincere, stand for justice, most importantly be honest with everything and everyone. We just have to practice it in our day-to-day life to reach to their levels.

How about you? What is your status regarding the matter above? Keep pondering...

TWO

FACE TO FACE WITH THE JOY STEALER

An attitude of complaining or grumbling is the biggest among all the joy stealers in life, as far as my knowledge is concerned. If we observe the faces of people, we will find them grumpy and ugly when they are complaining or grumbling about something or someone. When I was young, my aunt used to tell me: "*Go and see yourself in the mirror, how you look when you scream grumbling about something*".

And after the period, when I actually realize how I would be looking while complaining, I would feel ashamed of myself. But a question popped up in my mind as I was thinking about this grumbling attitude – ***"Why on earth do we complain or grumble?"***

I understand, it is good to raise one's voice against something wrong that we see but that's not what we are focusing on here.

If we closely observe our fellow humans, then we will find them complaining a lot of times at a particular time. There is a survey which tells that the average person complains 30 times a day. I was shocked to know that. Another article that I was reading says, "*the average adult complains for nine minutes approximately a day*". That's astounding!

"Do everything without grumbling or disputing, so that you may become blameless and pure..." This is what the Bible speaks of grumbling.

So, it means that, if we grumble, we are guilty. The attitude of complaining or grumbling is sinful.

- *But why is it so?*
- *Why doesn't God like mankind to grumble?*

I found the literal meaning of the word "***complainer***" in Greek is – "***one who is discontented with his lot in life.***" If I have to explain it in a simpler way, then a grumbler or complainer doesn't accept things that happen or the situations he or she is in and ultimately stays unhappy and grumpy all the time.

Coming back to the same question that evolved in my mind earlier: "*Why do we grumble or complain in the first place?*" "*What is the psychology behind complaining?*"

I found ***SEVEN*** such reasons which I have explained as under:

1. ***Dissatisfaction and Discontentment***: The first reason behind why we grumble, according to me is, when we are dissatisfied or not content with something that we receive or have in life. We grumble, complain and murmur showing our displeasure or annoyance. For example, I always grumble when my wife brings the parents of her students to our house.
2. ***Displaying Superiority***:
   Sometimes we grumble and complain of things or surroundings or rules, by displaying our superiority with regards to our knowledge of the matter more than others. "*He didn't understand the situation well at the time of crisis*" – this is a complaining statement made about someone else to depict that, "*I am more mature than him and I could have handled things better*".
3. ***Unwillingness and Excuses***: Most of the time when we are unwilling to do something, we give excuses in the form of complaining or grumbling about things or people. When children don't want to go to school, they either complain about stomachaches or about friends bullying them or about bad weather etc. Similarly, we adults grumble to ourselves when we skip going to the office due to our sheer unwillingness.
4. ***To Control Over***: We tend to complain or grumble pointing fingers at others to control people's minds. We provoke others to shift their allegiances to someone by complaining about or demeaning him or her. We find many such instances in corporate sectors and politics. Mudslinging is the weapon used to take control over a mass using grumbling as fuel.
5. ***Sense of Insecurity***: I have a colleague who is always irritable about everything and everyone, complaining about this or that all the time. And the clear reason behind this behaviour is, drawing the attention of all, as he feels insecure about his limited knowledge or lack of education.

6. ***In the defense of***: As humans, we complain about situations, circumstances or even the people around us many times to save ourselves from punishment or correction. For example, when students are asked to explain their delays to class, they usually complain about traffic or bus or something even vague to save themselves from the corrective measures impending against them.
7. ***Out of Habit***: Sometimes, out of habit, we grumble and become critical about everything that we receive or see or about people. This attitude becomes our way of leading life. It becomes a habit for some people, so to speak.

In my life, I have many more reasons to complain, stay grumpy and grumble all the time... and I have done so in my past, if not by raising my voice or protesting, but definitely in my heart and mind.

However, my life changed when I started to learn ***accepting*** things around me instead of allowing the joy stealer to overpower me. ***Focussing on God's goodness*** and ***thanking Him for all*** that HE has been doing in my life, transformed my mind and I started leading my life with a new mindset.

Friends! Be Thankful to God for whatever we have because that is the only antidote to cure the disease of complaining and grumbling.

THREE

ABUSING THE POWER OF FREEDOM

I was wondering, which are the various elements or thought processes in the world that gives us the power of freedom that we ultimately abuse or manipulate or misuse. And I found quite a number of things that allow us this *Power of Freedom*. I would love to talk about them one after the other.

LEFT ALL ALONE

- *Have you ever stayed all alone at home?*
- *What do you do when you are all alone?*
- *Do you do things which are allowable or permissible when your family members are around? or do you just freak out?*
- *Do you roam around naked (nothing to care about) in the house?*
- *Do you wait for that time when you can be left alone in the house so that you can accomplish your mischievous acts?*

The question is: ***"Why do we choose to do what we do?"***

On numerous occasions, I have stayed, all alone in my house, and that is the time I feel I have all the powers of this earth. That is the time when I feel, I can do everything that I want to as there's no one to watch me or instruct me or interfere in my matter or obstruct me. I feel I have all the freedom I can ever have at that particular moment of my aloneness. But that is the time I was put to test – <u>*The Test of Utilizing my Freedom*</u>.

No elders or parents would leave a kid alone in the house because they know that they are not mature enough to utilize their freedom. They can even put themselves in great danger. So, they were not given that liberty or freedom to stay alone at home.

My uncle who is also the founder of the organization I formerly worked at, always said one thing: *"I don't like tying you up with rules and regulations or being police around you, but allow you the freedom to grow and explore yourself within this organization with diligence and sincerity."*

But somewhere we lack to handle that power of freedom bestowed on or entrusted to us. I have failed at it many times, I won't lie. And I know we all fail at some point of time in our lives when we were left all alone.

The Bible says in Proverbs 18:1 – "***Whoever isolates himself seeks his own desire; he breaks out against all sound judgment.***"

DARKNESS/IN SECRET

By darkness, I mean the opportunity of not being caught or seen. This is actually quite similar to being left all alone but there's a difference here which I will further explain.

Let us look at a simple example:

Let us suppose, in a hall where many are celebrating an occasion and the parents of a boy have barred him not to tease the small girl of another couple. But unfortunately, there is a power cut and the hall became pitch dark for two minutes. And that darkness gave the boy the power of freedom and he went and pinched the cheeks of that little girl, to which she started squealing aloud. The boy would not have been punished severely by his parents if he would have obeyed his parents and would not have misused that momentary freedom he got because of darkness.

Thieves get that power of freedom when it is night or dark. Trust me, things that are done in darkness or undercover are never a righteous or pious one. Bribes are always given under the table or in secret.

Are we waiting for the lights to be switched off so that we can misuse the power of freedom we get because of that darkness? *Keep pondering.*

The Bible says in John 3:20 – "***Everyone who does evil hates the light, and will not come into the light for fear that their deeds will be exposed.***"

MONEY/WEALTH

Money gives purchasing power as well as the power of freedom to its owner. And mostly, they misuse it.

I remember, when I used to get a small salary, my monthly budget was small obviously and above that my desire to acquire things was lesser. But when I got a good amount of money at the beginning of the month, I felt that power of freedom to buy so many other things which I never used to think of. Don't think that I am talking about necessary items needed at home. I am talking about useless things which I buy sometimes and regret later on.

In most of the lower-middle-class families, you would find them struggling after the 25th of every month. Why? Because they used up their money lavishly using their power of freedom in the beginning and have nothing or significantly less money to buy the essentials for the last fourth or five days.

Hilarious???

But that is the truth.

The Bible says very interestingly in Proverbs 17:16 – ***"Why should fools have money in hand to buy wisdom, when they are not able to understand it?"***

If I go on like this, I can find many such things that allow us **complete freedom**, either for some time or forever. Like the gift of FREEWILL, the ***Power of Freedom*** is also attached with a series of responsibilities to it which are required to be carried out in a better way and not misused it.

Whether in our home among all the family members, within the marital boundary, or at our workplace, we get that power of freedom in our hands to exercise it. *Do we use them wisely or misuse them for selfish desires and addictions?*

Remember: ***"The abuse of liberty leads to bondage, the bondage of sin."***

FOUR
THE POWER OF WORDS

It was a cold December evening. I was lying on my bed with fever. I was feeling cold and very uncomfortable when my wife covered me with a thick blanket and gave me hot water bag to keep inside the blanket. After some time, I felt warm and much better. I realized how important warmth is to our body. It made me feel so comfortable.

My mind just took me to ponder about the words we speak. The word has power and it never comes back to us void. I always give the instance of my former boss Rev. Samson Nag who used to tell me one thing,

"Chiradeep, think ten times before you speak out; because once the words are out, they cannot be taken back and each word works either in a positive or negative way."

The question that emerges here is: What are the effects of the words that we speak? Have we ever thought about it? I had to brainstorm a bit to arrive at the answer to this question.

Effects of Our Words

Comforts & Heals: I know a doctor who owns a hospital in Cuttack. The patients of that hospital say that when the doctor speaks to us, we get cured and feel warm even before the treatment starts.

Proverbs 16:24 say that – *"Pleasant words are like a honeycomb, sweet and delightful to the soul and healing to the body."* How beautiful will it be when we speak and people get healed and comforted? But usually, it doesn't happen.

Hurts & Kills Emotions: Have you heard of the phrase: "*Character assassination?*" That's possible only through our powerful words when we gossip about a person behind him or her. Words of discouragement, defaming, and accusing can hurt the person at the receiving end.

I am very sensitive to the words that are spoken to me or what I have done. It affects me a lot. I feel troubled. I get hurt. Sometimes I have seen people pretend to be unaffected by the hurtful words of others but I am sure they would be definitely thinking about the words spoken to them when they are all alone by themselves.

If words have the power to stimulate, and stir our emotions of love, lust, and desire then it has the power to hurt and kill our emotions and enthusiasm to a very greater extent.

Regulates Anger: The Bible says, in Proverb 15:1, "*A gentle answer turns away wrath, but a harsh word stirs up anger.*" We all know when a husband is angry and the wife speaks gently to him instead of his hurtful words, his anger calms down after seeing her behaviour towards him. So many times, I had felt guilty for shouting at somebody in anger when he or she responded to me gently. Similarly, we get angry when we hear harsh words from the other party.

Hence, it is necessary to remember that the words that we utter can make somebody angry or calm him/her down because words regulate the emotion of anger.

Changes Perceptions: An article titled 'Words Have Power' by Jack Schafer on Psychology Today explains: "*Words cannot change reality, but they can change how people perceive reality. Words create filters through which people view the world around them. A single word can make the difference between liking a person and disliking that person.*"

If we characterize somebody with our words, we attach a tag to that person and people's perceptions get set accordingly for that particular person.

To cite an example: when somebody talks about a woman and says that "*She is a bitch*" the people around form an image of that particular woman. But when somebody else really tries to know her personally and finds her good then his or her old perception of that woman will change definitely.

So, we need to be careful when we judge and give different names to other persons knowing only a few facts about them.

Stirs up Dissension: I always feel that if we all can think ten times before we speak then we could stop many possible fatal incidences. There are many occasions where words have been destructive and have stirred up riots. History says that big riots have been stirred up just from small arguments between two friends. These days it's very common when people share words of hate or hate speeches through WhatsApp, Facebook, Twitter etc.

Affects Mind Negatively: Another article that I was reading in a magazine called 'Psychology Today', it says, *"If you vocalize your negativity, or even slightly frown when you say* ***"NO"*** *more stress chemicals will be released, not only in your brain but in the listener's brain as well."*

The listener will experience increased anxiety and irritability, thus undermining cooperation and trust." I felt extremely guilty reading this. So many times, I had said, "NO" to many people in anger or denied people of something and by doing so I must have affected mine as well as my listener's mind negatively. I might resolve that I will respond with positive affirmations henceforth. But when I read the article further, I found some worrisome facts which I am quoting here as well.

"When doctors and therapists teach patients to turn negative thoughts and worries into positive affirmations, the communication process improves and the patient regains self-control and confidence. But there's a problem: the brain barely responds to our positive words and thoughts. They're not a threat to our survival, so the brain doesn't need to respond as rapidly as it does to negative thoughts and words."

Now we can understand how important it is for us to speak positively.

In my life, I take pride in the fact that, I am very good at talking, putting my messages across and motivating someone I talk to but I am scared of one thing when I think of this verse in Proverbs 16:23: ***"The hearts of the wise make their mouths prudent, and their lips promote instruction."*** This makes me question myself: '*Does my mouth talk sense?*' '*Do I utter prudent words all the time?*' '*Do my lips promote instructions?*'

A wise king says in Proverbs 10:19, ***"sin is not absent in many words..."*** That alarms me and makes me think... Am I not committing any sin with the words, 'the many words' I use?

Let's consider and be mindful of the words we utter towards people... Do we add value when we speak out or cast shadows? How can the stream water be sweet and bitter at the same time? Pondering this thought is essential.

FIVE

THE DIFFERENCE BETWEEN THE WILD FLOWERS AND THE FLOWERS IN A GARDEN

A few years back, one of my very close friends revealed that she used to like me a lot and even have feelings for me presently (the time she revealed her feelings). But it was also true that she was happily married to her husband for years together. She could reveal her heart because she was clean in her heart and confirmed her dedication and love for her husband. But she went on to ask me a question that made me ponder on it, seeking an answer to that question.

"Why does God give that feeling of love in our hearts for someone very special but doesn't give the scope to culminate it?"

And I quite relate to that question as I have come across many beautiful relationships where I've felt to be drifting away though I have managed to get back on track. But this question still slithers in my mind and heart even today without having a proper answer to it. In fact, whenever I try to look for a proper answer to that question more questions are formed in my mind:

- ***Are connections bad?*** Probably, I will outnumber everyone in having connections with so many.
- ***Is it better to avoid making friends?*** I have never learnt avoiding or ignoring any human who interests me or who extends a hand towards me.
- ***Are emotions supposed to be suppressed?*** I am so outright honest with my feelings that I haven't learnt the skills to suppress my feelings at all.
- ***Is it good to pretend that everything is alright?*** Not at all, I really can't pretend and be alright. And the last question is a deadly one...
- ***Is drawing a line necessary?*** Absolutely!

Relationships are so beautiful that we build with people irrespective of their genders. But ironically, it is absolutely necessary for us to draw a line when we are supposed to. I would like to confess, sometimes I hate to draw a line with someone I love so much. But I just force myself to do so...

Why is it necessary? Why do I not have the scope or freedom to express my love for just anyone irrespective of their statuses (of whatever kind)? WHY???

I will give you a mental picture which might help you to understand why it is necessary to draw a line in relationships...

> *"When we take a walk in the woods, or roads, or a field we find many beautiful flowers across the path blooming and smiling at us. They grow erratically with freedom. They look good, no doubt about it but they succumb to their end without proper care and attention because they are stray, far from a caretaker. Usually, those who walk across them, pluck them or uproot them from the source of their life and nourishment.*
>
> *Whereas, if we look at the flowers in a garden, they bloom with pride and are well taken care of by someone who is attentive to them, not necessarily an able gardener or farmer."*

Relationships that we make are like those beautiful flowers blooming with different colours and beauty. But they all look beautiful, protected and safe within a boundary drawn with godly standards.

The Bible says in Proverbs 16:32, ***"Better a patient person than a warrior, one with self-control than one who takes a city."*** And a person with self-control draws a line and creates a beautiful garden.

How about bringing those wild flowers into the garden within a boundary? They will look beautiful within those lines as well.

Actually, our fallen nature makes things complicated. And God, probably doesn't allow us to be disorderly and stray because He knows, the more we are allowed, the more perverse we will be in our behaviour and life. Why can't we be of a clean mind, and keep beautiful friendships all around?

Friends! Let's enjoy the relationships that we make within a permissive line drawn for the safety and lasting of those relationships.

SIX

ARE YOU ADAPTING OR FORCED LIVING?

"Modification of an organism or its parts that makes it more fit for existence under the conditions of its environment: a heritable physical or behavioural trait that serves a specific function and improves an organism's fitness or survival." - Merriam-Webster

The chapter of adaptation in the school text book used to be my favourite when I was a kid. I used to enjoy studying about the animals and birds who try their best to adapt to the situation or environment they are in. And those who are successful in the process of adaptation survive and live on, but the others face death.

Isn't it the same way about us who try to fit into a social setup, a family, a college, or a workplace? We try to get accustomed or adapted to the rules, the way of living and the thinking of the people in that setup. And after a certain period of time, we become one of them. Sometimes it works the other way around. The individual who comes into a group of people influences so much they or get adapted to his or her ways. Whichever way it is, adaptation brings peace and harmony.

On the other hand, when we try to force ourselves to fit into a group or family or gathering either we struggle to continue for some time or simply quit or stay happy the rest of our lives. The simple fact is, when we don't have the desire to adapt, we can't adapt. When we can't adapt, we force and pretend. At some point in time, we even rebel against our given environment or situation. Life becomes really tough for the person resisting adapt.

That's why Jennifer Guttman Psy.D. says rightly, "*Adaptation is a natural next step in personal growth.*"

The most common example that I can give is about a newlywed bride who comes to a new family. The quicker she mingles or adapts to the family, the easier it becomes for her to live amidst them. Though adaptation should happen both ways. Frictions are inevitable when we interact with one another, but there won't be any conflicts if there're people adapting to each other quickly.

There are a few quick symptom trackers to analyse a person adapting or force living. A person who finds it easy to take a NO from the other person, he or she is adaptable or adapting. But when he or she makes a fuss out of everything, is not ready to adapt or accept the situation around him or her. If it continues for over a period of time, he or she leads his/her life forcibly. Insecurity, grumbling and complaining are major indicators of a person force-living instead of adapting in a family or workplace or any other social group. Force-living always brings unhappiness and frustration but adaption brings togetherness and ownership.

A word of caution before I end this article: ***Always try to get adapted to things that are positive, good and godly because adapting to evil is quicker and dangerous.***

So, friends! Are you adapting well or struggling and force-living? Keep pondering...

ᑭᑭᑭ

SEVEN

MEANINGLESS! MEANINGLESS!

One day suddenly, I felt, life is meaningless and whatever I have achieved or doing has no meaning. Maybe, you feel the same as I do, at times. This can happen out of nowhere, for no apparent reason. But it is necessary to understand why and when it happens.

Meaninglessness in life or anything we do or in any situation we are in comes when we are unable to find value in our life or the things we do. It comes when we feel insignificant in this huge wide world. It comes when failure lives in our house as a permanent member.

I find, lack of THREE very important factors within us which brings the sense of meaninglessness. They are the short form of the word IMPORTANT – **IMP**.

Let's get into a brief analysis of IMP for clear understanding of the matter.

Lack ofINTEREST: I find it funny when I hear everything a person says yet I fail to remember anything he said. The reading of the text or hearing the speech or the message directed towards me becomes meaningless when I don't conceive it because of my lack of interest in them. When I don't have the curiosity of knowing or understanding something, I lose to understand the very meaning of it as well.

Lack ofMOTIVATION: I usually avoid leadership training or conferences these days. The reason I avoid to attending those seminars is very simple... I find them meaningless when I don't have the scope to implement what I learn theoretically in those seminars. The scope to apply what you learn gives you a motivation to do it. And I don't have that motivation so I find it meaningless for me. I really love it, I have interest in those speeches and training modules. I understand the purpose behind, yet I don't have the motivation behind it.

Sometimes, in life, when we lack motivation, we fail to understand how to lead it.

Lack ofPURPOSE: Just imagine, if your children go to schools or colleges with the sole purpose of finding a good life partner then the whole concept of education becomes meaningless. When the purpose of what we are doing or why we are living is not known or understood by us then we run errands meaninglessly and a time comes when we lose motivation and interest to do anything or find life meaningless to live. The purpose of life is the foundation of living it meaningfully and without it, we perish.

All the above THREE words or factors seem very similar to each other but they have different connotations if we study them carefully. ***Interest*** gives us the feeling to attempt something, ***Motivation*** helps us to move forward with the same that interests us and ***Purpose*** directs us to move forward in the right path to accomplish what we are motivated about. There is no ranking or order of these three factors, called **IMP.** They are all part of the same system which makes our life beautiful and meaningful whether it is something that we do in our day to day lives or cater to the needs of our mental faculties or about our spiritual matters.

There is one Bible verse which I always love to quote while explaining the topics concerning life. That's in Proverbs 20:5, which reads,

"The purpose in a man's heart is like deep water, but a man of understanding will draw it out."

At times, when we struggle to find the meaning of our life, we need to sit down and meditate on God's goodness and His ways of dealing with people. He works amazingly and mysteriously. The more we go deeper diving down into the matters of our soul and eternity, the more we will draw out, that are beautiful, mysterious and meaningful for us. That happens when we are wise enough to do.

But the question is who is then wise or man of understanding? The Bible again says in Proverbs 9:10,

"The reverent fear of the Lord that is, worshipping Him and regarding Him as truly awesome is the beginning and the preeminent part of knowledge [its starting point and its essence];"

When we acknowledge God in our life, we gain knowledge and become wise. And when we become wise and men of understanding we get to go deep down to comprehend the purpose of life, ultimately finding the meaning of life and living it to the fullest.

EIGHT

REEVALUATING WHILE LOCKED-DOWN

I have heard from my elders how they went into a situation like this, '***Lockdown***' during the war against Pakistan and during the World Wars. But this time, it's a little different. We don't have to switch off the lights, stay hiding inside our rooms, stop looking outside popping our heads out through the window, wondering if the bombs will fall on us and so on... But sometimes, we so underestimate the gravity and severity of a situation that we behave so funny and childish. When death rates are constantly rising every moment and there are 100% chances of financial crash-down worldwide we are worrying only about a ***lockdown***.

It was so funny to see how people so quickly reacted when the announcement about a complete lockdown situation was made by our P.M.:

- *"How boring it will be staying at home for so long?"*
- *"We can't go out to meet our friends..."*
- *"We have to do all the household works as maids won't be available..."*
- *"How will we spend our times all day?"*
- *"I have planned to watch Netflix all day long..."*
- *"It's nothing more than imprisonment..."*
- *"What will we eat? Same food again and again?"*

All these we could update on *Facebook*, *WhatsApp* and *Instagram* statuses, expressing our irritation and worries because we are still not hit by Covid19 directly. We are still on *listening and reading the news mode.* God forbid, once one of our family members gets infected, we will surely forget how to express or react.

Am I out of these lot? No way... I am part of the same crowd who tends to get bored and irritated. Although my answer was different when someone asked me seeing me loitering outside my room, "Bored???"

I shook my head and said, "NO!! I am quite habituated with this lockdown situation from the very beginning of life."

The person who asked me, understood what I meant and walked away acknowledging my response.

YET!!!

I was wondering – '*What lockdown means to me?*'

1. Retrieving what I have lost: Suddenly when I have a lot of time at my disposal, I was happily scrolling away the pages of Pinterest on my phone and I came across an image of a beautiful paper-art. I felt an urge rekindled to let my fingers create something similar to what I saw. I cursed myself for not foreseeing this situation and buy colours, brushes and marble papers for paper-arts and paintings. I remember, how much I used to paint and draw pictures when I was a student. I had lost everything with an excuse of being busy in life.

I have made up my mind, that I am going to retrieve everything that I have lost and this lockdown will help me to give a kick start till I live on this earth.

2. Recreating what I have left unfinished and undone: I am known as a motivator and a person who initiates. But sadly, I want to confess that I am not good at continuing things or finishing it. I started to write a book, I started to plan for studying a Biblical Counselling Course, paid for it as well... I started to plan for a music album... Urgh! I have kept everything pending, unfinished and undone.

I pray, "***God, give me that enthusiasm to recreate all that I have left unfinished and undone utilizing these period of lockdown***".

3. Reinstating what I have kept detached: Yesterday, my cousin sister requested me to give her time so that she could connect with four of our families to see, talk and pray with each other considering the situation we have been facing now. The time was fixed and we had little problem with network but finally we could gather to have a video chat with each other, laugh, smile and ultimately pray for all the people suffering around the globe. And in the night while on my bed, resting my head on the pillow I was thinking, "*Why I am so detached with all? I am not a person like this... why do I stay away from people for a year or so?*"

Everyone knows how I build relationships. And that's what I love to do – *investing my time in people's lives.* I was feeling so uncomfortable when I was passive about this favourite thing that I love to do... But I did start connecting with people again, building new relationships and restoring the older ones during this lockdown period.

Trust me, I am going to reinstate every friendship, relationship that I have detached myself from.

4. Rearranging what I have left messy: Indiscipline, distractions and waywardness bring down someone into utter chaos and mess. For last two or three years I allowed myself to be in a mess

Reasons? I cannot explain.

I might justify my life being not as bad as others, not as much in the mess as others but my heart knows it should not be like this anyway.

Okay! So, I have a lot of time to repair, rearrange, reorganize my mess and bring it back on track by re-surrendering myself in His divine care. Surrendering life to God doesn't mean resting peacefully...but to rework all the more and strive to convert my mess, into a mesmerizing whole.

5. Reprioritizing what I have ignored: God and the purpose He has in and through my life is my priority. I confess, I have kind of ignored it for last couple of years. I don't want to give excuses by blaming my illness or life situations. I understand, I might be faltering yet God does and will pull me back every time I go astray but I am desperately seeking His strength to help me reprioritize and stay focus on Him and the purpose that He has for me while I am alive in this world.

This lockdown gives me enough time to pray and gain strength from Him to see the people and their needs through His eyes, His perspective. My heart moves with compassion when I look at those people suffering and dying without fulfilling life's eternal purpose. My heart cries. This lockdown made me kneel down on my knees and pray for them and feel for them which I could not have done it if I would have been in a Covid19-less normal situation.

Lockdown means, a lot of time for me to work on all the above ***5 RE's*** along with whatever emergency work that I could do from home or by going to the office as I live in the same campus where my office is located. You might think these points are not relatable to you, especially the last ***RE***, but I know they are. You never know, how devastating the post Covid19 period will be than the present state of affairs due to Corona-virus.

So, let this '***Lockdown Period***' be the most important period of your life apart from all the enjoyment and entertainment that you have planned, assuming you and I would survive and beat Covid19... Uhhmmm

Stay at home and keep pondering on ***5 RE's***...

NINE

ARE YOU A TARGET OF GOSSIP AND RUMOUR?

The synonyms of the word '***Rumour***' are *comment, news, fabrication, report, falsehood, scandal, gossip, story, hearsay, suggestion, hoax, tale, whisper, word, lie, innuendo etc.*

There were 16 such words above that were quite relevant to the word '***Rumour***', but out of those 16 words, 10 are extremely negative. All the previously published articles have explained about this topic in detail. But we all agree that ***rumour*** never does any good to the gossip mongers or to the victim of the same.

I was wondering about the person who becomes the topic of discussion among many, about whom the rumour is spread, who is blamed and accused indirectly instead of talking or addressing the person face to face. Just imagine how hurtful it is to be the topic of discussion for no reason. Just imagine how the person must be leading his or her life when he or she knows that there are people talking behind their back in a faulty manner.

A rumour about someone who is innocent can cause majorly **four damages** to that person:

1. ***It destroys his/her REPUTATION***
2. ***It pushes him/her into NEEDLESS MENTAL STRESS***
3. ***It makes him/her to SELF-ALIENATE from own people even***
4. ***It stops his/her PROGRESS for SOMETIME or for LIFETIME***

But I want to focus on the part where we can get out of this phase of being the target of rumours and gossips and live our life as we, our family and our God intended for us.

I am very much aware of the rumours and gossips that have been spreading around in our community concerning my inability, my sickness and the assumptions they cook out of them.

Am I *affected* **by it?**

Yes, of course! I feel my reputation is spoiled, I avoid to face certain people in my life, I avoid talking to people over the phone, I suffer from regrets and mental stress... BUT I never allowed them to stop me from moving ahead...

Why and how?

'How to handle rumours when we are the target?' – I have **FIVE solid steps** that I follow and can help all of us to deal with rumours and gossips when we are the victims of it.

1. Step back: Stepping back from the situation and the negative emotions surrounding us, temporarily help us big time. When the fire flares in front of us, we step back reflexively before we plan to control it. It is the same method that we need to follow when we face the flares of rumours and gossips trying to burn our reputation. Acting on our negative emotions like revenge and anger can cause more problems to us, so it is wise for us to step back for some time, till our negative emotions towards the person or the whole situation dies down.

This stepping back has always helped me to reorganize my emotions and reacting impulsively has always put me into shame and disgust. Take my words... I have gone through it.

2. Forgive and forget: When we step back, we plan to deal with the situation. We struggle to be at peace at the memory, the hurts haunt us. We might feel that avenging the person who wronged us or seeing them punished would give us peace of mind. But that's not the truth. A negative feeling won't be eradicated with another negative act. Only forgiving and forgetting the person who had done wrong to us with the help from above divinely can actually calms our hearts and minds down.

Today, I was talking to someone who wants to see her perpetrators punished in her presence so that she can have peace. But I lovingly made her understand that's not how someone can attain peace. It is only forgiving the person who wronged us, can allow God to work within us and we can have peace that is beyond human understanding.

3. **De-identifying from the situation**: We have a habit of identifying ourselves or relating to the situation very quickly or impulsively. That always pulls us behind. A rumour is an act of a person who is flawed. Though we are not perfect, yet we need to remember that someone else's remark or the remarks of people don't certify our characters. So why to identify or recognize the situation as a reflection of us or our characters? De-identifying from the situation is absolutely fantastic to deal well with the rumours and gossips against us.

4. **Refocus and Look at the bigger picture**: I always try to apply this step in my life. My future doesn't depend on what people think or say about me. I am solely responsible for my life, no one else. It is only God who can make me or break me. I know this truth yet at times I struggle because of what people talk behind me, close ones spread rumours about me. I falter yet, try to shift my focus ahead instead of looking here and there.

Looking at the bigger picture of our life is important instead of dwelling in the mess created by some gossip and rumour mongers.

5. **Respond to the person who wronged us**: This step is optional. This step can be taken when we have come out of the mess completely and have built ourselves to help others going through such difficulties. We can go up to the person who wronged us or spread rumours about us and explain how hurtful what he or she did was to us. It is always good to let the person know how it feels. But this step can be avoided if we are not confident enough to face the man or woman who caused us so much pain.

Are you a target of gossip and rumour, today? I want to encourage all of you to follow the above mentioned steps. I would also urge you to take your hurts and scars to God who would heal you and fill your heart with His peace.

While closing this article, I want to address the people who knowingly or unknowingly become the medium of a rumour or lie about someone who is innocent. I will just quote Philippians 4:8 from the Bible for them where it instructs to think and understand about a few attributes that are very essential for our as well as the welfare of others... And in that list '*following what is true*' is mentioned first.

"Finally, brothers and sisters, whatever is true, whatever is noble, whatever is right, whatever is pure, whatever is lovely, whatever is admirable—if anything is excellent or praiseworthy—think about such things."

Friends! Let's choose TRUTH over *LIES*. Let's turn our ears away from rumours and strive to search and research the Truth about everything and everyone. Let's not heed a rumour and participate in a gossip journey which can be hurtful to someone who's innocent. Stay watchful and careful of rumour and gossips.

TEN

POUR VINEGAR TO HEAL, NOT TO KILL

Vinegar is an extremely important ingredient in some of the oldest as well as the newest food items. I remember, when I was a small kid, I used to watch my grandma making all kinds of Achaar (pickle). She used to soak all the raw mangos, lemons, berries etc., in the vinegar and then dry them in the sun. Afterwards, she would cook them into different kinds of pickles according to the fruits – Mango pickle, Berry pickle, Lemon pickle and so on.

When I grew up, I understood the use of vinegar to marinate raw meat and then cook them after some time. And when I visited restaurants, I found vinegar with green chillies soaked in a bottle which are usually used as sauces or added flavour to soup and other dishes as salt, pepper etc.

When I started taking interest in cooking, soya sauce and vinegar were my favourites. As I know they would cover up my follies if any and bring the taste in them.

I was curious to know about the various uses of vinegar in our life and I was shocked to find them in numerous amounts when I browsed the internet. I have mentioned a few below:

- Vinegar, as we know, is an effective preservative. It works by making the food more acidic, which deactivates its enzymes and kills any bacteria in the food that may cause spoilage.
- Vinegar has anti-bacterial properties because of which it helps as a deodorizer.
- Vinegar is used in food items for various purposes. It is used in salad dressings. It is used to marinate meat to add flavour to the fry or curry or

any dish that we try to prepare.

- Vinegar is claimed to help diabetics control their blood sugar levels.
- Some test tube studies say that vinegar can kill cancer cells.
- Vinegar is a natural cleaning agent. It also helps to wash fruits and vegetables clean. It helps in cleaning our skins as well. Many people use it during bath too. Vinegar can be used like this in varied cleaning purposes because of its antibacterial properties.
- Vinegar sometimes is recommended as help to weight loss because it may help you feel full.
- Vinegar neutralizes the sting of minor burns and helps them heal more quickly by reducing the swelling. It also helps to cure pimples and acne.

The list can just go on and on... But there's a glitch in it.

As I was discussing the uses of vinegar with my colleague in the office today, he was saying that they usually marinate meat with a spoon as vinegar might burn the skin. Vinegar helps as a mouthwash but if we use it without knowing how to use it then vinegar use would be fatal than useful. We can not chew anything with our teeth if we use raw vinegar as a mouthwash.

The time, the quality and the quantity are very essential in every aspect of our life which we need to understand. If we don't understand it then we suffer or let others suffer.

There's a Bible verse in Proverbs 25:20 which made me smile and also gave me wisdom. It reads, "***...like vinegar poured on a wound, is one who sings songs to a heavy heart***".

Remember? Above we saw how vinegar helps the wound to heal quickly but if it is not used in accordance with the proper method of usage by keeping the quality, quantity and time then the suffering of the wounded would be extreme.

A question popped up in my mind, "*Does my counselling sometimes feel like vinegar on the wound to the one hurting*?"

Sometimes parents and elders taunt their younger ones to correct them. It is definitely helpful at times while they reprimand but when it is done regularly as a habit then it spoils everything.

Be careful! Pour vinegar to heal, not to kill.

ELEVEN

MY RESPONSE VALIDATES MY LISTENING SKILLS

Have you ever wondered why we have two ears? Usually, people say – *"so that we can listen more and talk less."* That's alright but that's not the reason why we have been created with two ears on both sides of our head.

We have two ears so that we can understand the ***direction of the noise***, our ***hearing ability widens***, ***clarity of what we hear increases***, the ***strain of loud noise is reduced or divided*** between our two ears. And to help our ears to listen more effectively we have got two eyes as well, which help us to see, read, understand and focus on the person and his/her expressions. But sadly, despite having two ears and two eyes we often fail to listen to others.

I have heard many telling me that I am a good listener, but a few others from my close bunch think, that I am not. So, when I decided to write on the topic of listening, I started weighing my art of listening first. I found a few startling facts about myself which are as follows:

1. I am patient enough listening to a stranger.
2. I am very calm and have listened to someone who's angry, has control and authority over me.
3. I am impatient to listen to something which I have heard repeatedly from a person many times.
4. I am irritated and don't like to listen when I am exhausted and tired.

5. I am impatient and don't like to listen attentively to a person who's under my control and authority.
6. I ask my family members and close relatives to wait.
7. I listen to the person who interests me more over others.

And the findings can go on and on... But this contemplation helped me to understand my status regarding "***listening***" to others which made me understand that, "***Listening***" is a character when a person is inherently a good listener and it is an art to be learned over the years when a person can train himself or herself to listen to people and their hearts deliberately but effectively.

I concluded after a thorough introspection that, I have an inherent character of empathising with people, so I listen to them yet, I still have a lot of training required for myself to help me listen to the people carefully, skilfully and effectively.

Now, the next question popped up in my mind is – '***how to rate my listening skills?***'

I feel there are exactly three ways how I can rate my own listening skills...

- Feedback from the one I am listening to (the vulnerable one, the one in need, the counselled, etc.)
- Feedback from the one who stays along with me almost all the time (my spouse, friends, colleagues, etc.)
- Feedback from my inner being as I am the best person to know whether I have listened carefully or not

If you ask me regarding the basis of those feedbacks, then my answer would be they are based on my responses or the way I respond to people who need to be heard. Yes! each ***response of mine*** to the one who shares his/her heart with me ***validates my listening skills.***

Let me explain it little elaborately as under:

1. ***Listening attentively***: This is a very basic stage of listening. I think we all understand this very well. Our posture, eye contact, and interest in the matter or the person is important when we try to listen to someone who is in need of sharing. Paying attention needs time, patience and lots of compassion. A couple of my friends came up with a lot of beautiful scenarios to validate what I want to say here. They gave instances

explaining how our not being attentive to someone can jeopardize things around us. My response of being an attentive listener validates my skill and lets me pass stage one.

2. ***Listening to the emotions***: This is not a situation where we will just get two chairs: one will speak and another will listen. We have to listen through noises, through fits of anger, shouts and even sobs. When people are upset, angry, frustrated, disappointed or hurt, their tendency is to discuss their feelings with others so that they can *be released from their anguish which has been clouding their hearts and minds* for a long time. The scenario can be anywhere, within the family or professionally. However, if we simply look at them and shrug or respond by giving advice or by telling them what they did wrong, they won't feel any better and will probably feel worse after sharing their hearts with us. Because all they want is for us to validate their feelings by conveying our understanding to them, showing our sympathy or empathy; by letting them know that we are with them listening to them lovingly, without being judgemental of their feelings or behaviours. Here, my response of decoding those shouts and noises and venting explains my skills. Am I bouncing back or absorbing everything to comfort the hurting soul? Am I annoyed with the hyperactive person I am talking to or considerate enough to allow myself to be a punching bag for him or her to punch till he or she feels better?

   (*NOTE: **Emotional validation** is the process of learning about, understanding and expressing acceptance of another person's **emotional***)

3. ***Listening to silence***: Trust me, this is the most difficult one. Many times, I have heard the loud noise of silence which I tried to understand without listening to it. Sometimes, I don't get to hear the person weeping or talking hyperactively or even shouting or venting at me but all he or she does is to remain absolutely quiet or silent... I become clueless yet, I try to invade that silence and listen to it. All I can do is just ***notice*** as Aastha, a good friend did about her sister. She noticed carefully to find the reasons behind her sister being dull and depressed. Though, I agree that this is possible when the bonding is strong. It is not easily done when two people are strangers to each other and don't have much scope to see each other for a longer period. This is possible within a home scenario or between best friends etc. mostly. So, the more I listen to the silence of other people by noticing well, the more skilful I am. Noticing well is my response to someone's silence.

Nevertheless, at times, I find myself very helpless when I am unable to clearly listen and understand the person I care about and do everything possible to listen to him or her. When someone doesn't allow us to listen to him or her, it becomes difficult to listen. But I remind myself – ***God starts working from where I stop***.

So, how do you respond when you have someone in your presence to listen carefully?

TWELVE

HOW TO RESIST TEMPTATIONS?

Once, I asked a question to my near and dear ones: "*How do you tackle the temptations when you come across them?*" It is a broad question and cannot be elaborated in short. What I meant was – "*What is the first shield of protection you hold to resist the temptation you face?*" In fact, I went back to the same persons and asked this specific question and their replies were same. The replies were:

"I ask myself if I really can do without it. I take time."

"I increase my will... If I have to lose weight, then I determine not to eat Puchka...(Crispy Indian Snack)"

"Well... I give in to some and resist some.... I don't resist all temptations... and the ones I do, I use logic to resist..."

"Depends on my will power at that point of time and my state of mind... Sometimes I just give in and when I do – I try not to feel guilty... My shield is – distraction."

"I ask my loved ones to stop me from getting tempted. They remind me why at the first place I tried to stay away from that temptation itself."

"I will do just a prayer to God to help me through the situation..."

"Think of the consequences."

"I first think what will happen to my identity."

"Prayer – that's the key for me. Taking it to God."

"I will think if its really necessary for me..."

"I will rely on my sense of right and wrong.... The first thing I will remind myself that it's not the right thing to do... And I have this very bad habit of trying to be in everyone's good books... So I will be conscious of how will I look to others if

I do this..."

The replies were commendably honest and fabulous. I appreciate all those who have opened their hearts before me.

Now, let's get into a study of the word '***Temptation***'.

The web or Google dictionary defines it as: "*the desire to do something, especially something wrong or unwise.*" Hence, a temptation is always something WRONG that we fall into.

Vocabulary.com explains it as: "*Temptation is something you want to have or to do, even though you know you shouldn't.*" Hence, a temptation is wrong and we KNOW it while falling prey to it.

Wikipedia describes it as: "*Temptation is a desire to engage in short-term urges for enjoyment, that threatens long-term goals. It is the inclination to sin.*" So, a temptation can CAPTIVATE its prey.

There's one Christiananswers.net which defines it as: "*Temptation is common to all.*" So, a temptation is UNAVOIDABLE in life.

WOW!

We got to know some facts about the word ***Temptation*** whichI have mentioned above in the CAPITAL case.

Now the question arises, "*how to resist the temptations?*"

1. **Fleeing Away from it:** I loved a reply which goes like this, **"I take time"**. It is always safe when we take ourselves away from the temptations... from the place... from the object of temptations etc. Another reply was, **"Distraction"**. That is also a similar kind of strategy that keeps us away from the direct effects of temptation. The Bible instructs us: "flee from the youthful lusts", "flee for lives..." etc. So sometimes FLEEING AWAY from the area of temptation helps us to resist it because it is not very easy to resist it.
2. **Practice on a Daily Basis:** Another reply was, **"I increase my will or have a strong willpower..."**. Having a strong determination or willpower really helps us to resist temptations, but it is not at all easy as temptations are plenty and unavoidable in life. So how to increase our willpower? It's a daily affair... we need to consider many such elements in our life that weaken our willpower. Recognizing them and getting rid of them are important in our practice of being determined. So how do we do that? Avoid pornographic content, jokes, talks, erotica etc., if you are being tempted to indulge in sexual stuff. Instead cultivate a habit of reading good content, studying scriptures, staying in safe places, watching good

movies etc. Another thing we need to consider is with whom do we associate on a daily basis...? Who are our friends...? Peer pressure and friend circle are the biggest reasons that lead us to different kinds of temptations. They totter our willpower... so it is better to change our friend circles if they do not help us to resist the temptations. The Bible instructs, "Whatever is true, whatever is noble, whatever is right, whatever is pure, whatever is lovely, whatever is admirable—if anything is excellent or praiseworthy—think about such things." That helps a great deal for sure in strengthening our mind and will power.

3. **Be Accountable to Someone close:** Some time ago I decided that I would report everything I did to one of my sisters. It is not that she will instruct me or keep a check on me but that helps. It reminded me that if I have to tell her the truth about myself then I need to do what is right... It is not easy to do that but why not give it a try. One of the replies above was, "I ask my loved ones to stop me from getting tempted. They reminded me about why I tried to resist the temptation".
4. **Relying on a Greater Strength:** Two of the above replies were about "Praying to God" which is really very essential. The carnal desires are very natural and defeating them with carnal strength is daunting and sometimes impossible. So divine intervention always makes things easier for us. Prayer is the way we stay connected to our Creator God. Another reply was about relying on our conscience, on our sense of right and wrong... Staying connected to the divinity sharpens our conscience. We become sensitive to the wrong and right things in life... It becomes easier for us to differentiate between right and wrong. I remember one more scripture portion which says, "...when you are tempted, God will also provide a way out so that you can stand up under it". Wow! That's amazing! Our loving God is always ready to help us and show us a way out whenever we call on to Him.

In conclusion to my article, I would like to say that, the temptation is like an apple kept in front of you after you are starving for hours without eating anything. Before you think about your identity, about the consequences, about using your logic to resist you fall flat in the trap of temptations... It is not so easy to resist the temptations of life but take heart it is not impossible either. Somebody very close to my heart says, *There have been times in which I have yielded to temptations too, even after knowing God's standards fully well. Then the only way out is to confess and seek HIS forgiveness. As a reflection, I have always come to the conclusion that whenever I have given in to temptation, I have placed someone/something over and above God.*

Let's gather ourselves today, tighten our belt on the waist and stand firm to RESIST the temptation by considering all of the above.

"Can a man scoop fire into his lap without his clothes being burned?
Can a man walk on hot coals without his feet being scorched?
Proverbs 6:27-29"

ꝒꝒꝒ

THIRTEEN

ATTITUDE OF GIVING RECOGNITION

Recognition is necessary for a person to become motivated. I understand that doing things sincerely and responsibly, whether recognised or not, is a sign of integrity; however, recognition is critical at every stage of our lives.

I'm not going to write about receiving or expecting adulation from others. I'll discuss the proper ways or manners of recognising someone who deserves it.

"*Do not withhold good from those to whom it is due when it is in your power to do it,*" the Bible verse in Proverbs 3:27 warns us. It makes no difference whether it is something tangible or intangible, such as recognising someone who deserves it.

So, what are the proper ways or attitudes of '***not withholding***' due recognition from someone? This is explained by THREE such factors.

Timely: I've witnessed people postponing the act or event of recognizing or acknowledging someone. They either delay in the name of planning or keep the individual concerned waiting while making excuses for some nebulous reason. It is considered an insult or disrespect to someone if acknowledgement or recognition due to him is not given at the appropriate time, even if we try to patch up or make up for everything later. There is no substitute for the recognition that comes at the right time. The best recognition is given at the right time.

Genuinely: Even if the words are few, appreciating or recognizing someone with the right tone and spirit works. When the tone is off, flattery or more words of praise may not be effective. "He is Chiradeep, the backbone of our organization," one of my previous bosses used to say while introducing me. And I used to be irritated by his flattery. When I was alone with him, I used to request him not to introduce me that way. When we acknowledge or recognize someone, we must be genuine.

Impartially: When we recognize someone, we should always ask ourselves whether we recognized them genuinely and impartially. Genuineness and impartiality appear to be synonymous, but they are not. When there are more than two people to be acknowledged, the word impartial comes to the scene. Our recognition or appreciation for both individuals may be genuine, but they may be partial if we show undue favour to one over the other. Let me give you an example: two employees in an organisation. They both worked hard to complete a task together. Both were given the same amount of money as a reward, but the boss praised one more than the other. If I were in his shoes, I would feel very bad and disgusted.

The Bible says in James 2:9, "***if you show favouritism, you sin and are convicted by the law as lawbreakers***."

Friends, let's not be tired of recognising or acknowledging people who deserve it. Let's be prompt to do that timely, genuinely and impartially.

FOURTEEN

7 FACTORS TO RECONCILE WITH YOUR LOVED ONES AND RESTORE A BROKEN RELATIONSHIP

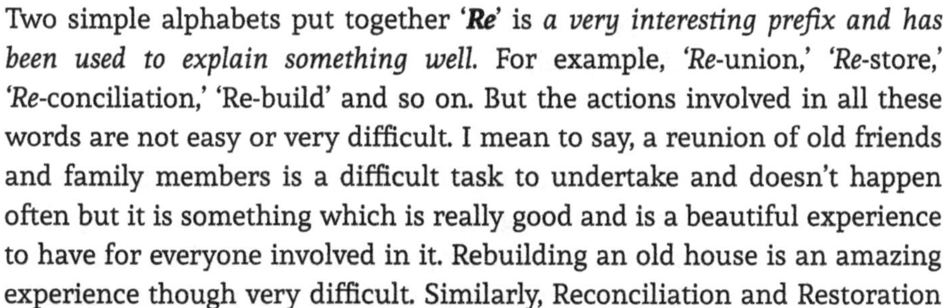

Two simple alphabets put together '***Re***' is *a very interesting prefix and has been used to explain something well.* For example, '*Re*-union,' '*Re*-store,' '*Re*-conciliation,' 'Re-build' and so on. But the actions involved in all these words are not easy or very difficult. I mean to say, a reunion of old friends and family members is a difficult task to undertake and doesn't happen often but it is something which is really good and is a beautiful experience to have for everyone involved in it. Rebuilding an old house is an amazing experience though very difficult. Similarly, Reconciliation and Restoration of broken relationships are utterly difficult.

One of my younger cousins calls me the '*Glue Man*,' as I try to keep everyone together despite our differences. Dissension and strain in any relationship are awful. Personally, I do not like to stay away or stop talking or communicating for long after a fight or difference of opinions. I try to keep the relationship on and on in every situation. But it is not something very easy at all times.

A good and healthy relationship is what gives us the strength and reason to live and survive. It is the only potion that prevents and cures loneliness, depression, distress and sadness. It has always helped us to find a way in life. A relationship gives us authority towards one another's lives. A relationship is the radar or rudder of our lifeboat. When a relationship is broken, we find ourselves in the middle of the sea, sinking down in the water inch by inch.

It is burdensome when we look around and find many broken relationships in the world today. Our heart aches when we see a home torn wide apart and shattered. It is so sad to see a child getting parted and divided physically, mentally and spiritually between two separated or divorced parents. It is so pathetic to witness the ageing parents who are being driven out of their homes by their children. It is terrible to see brothers fight for a piece of land and cut off their relationships with each other forever.

But the good news is there are many who are broken yet want to be united again with their loved ones. There are many husbands who want their wives to come back to their arms and many wives who are desperate to reconcile with their husbands. It's never too late to mend a broken relationship. It's never impossible to get back, reconcile and restore a strained relationship. It's never shameful to get back to your loved ones.

But the biggest difficulty that stands as a mountain before people today is, ***"HOW DO WE RECONCILE? HOW DO WE REBUILD? HOW DO WE RESTORE?"***

I have 7 very simple yet important factors that have always helped me in my life and will definitely help many to reconcile and rebuild a broken relationship and they are mentioned as under:

1. Feeling the Need:

A relationship can be restored only when we have the desire to reconcile and rebuild. Unless we have a longing to come together or unite together, we cannot think of rebuilding. For example, if I think "*She doesn't show any interest to reconcile*" then I would be sure that I am not ready to reconcile. When we feel the relationship with our loved ones needs to be restored because of our own needs then we know that we are ready to take a step forward towards restoration.

2. Taking the first step:

I have seen that in life, we always tend to expect the first initiation from the opposite party. I have also had the experience in my own life that if I want to reconcile then I have to take the first step. I can't expect somebody to come and give me a glass of water when I feel thirsty. I need to express my feelings or ask for a glass of water or get it myself. The process of reconciliation and rebuilding starts when we take the first initiation in response to our own needs.

3. Expecting Denial:

When we are on the verge of rebuilding and restoring, we should always be ready for denial in the beginning. The other person may not want to rebuild or reconcile initially. So, we should not be disappointed with her/his denial, we should be ready to face that and accept it in a very positive way.

4. Patience is the Key:

We should never lose our patience. We always need to remember that "*breaking is much easier than rebuilding.*" We need patience. We need perseverance. We have to keep coming again and again to reconcile. And one day when we succeed, we have to start rebuilding slowly.

5. A Humbling experience:

It is not easy to come again and again expecting a response to our invitation to reconcile and restore a strained relationship. It is a humbling experience. We need humility along with patience to break the wall between us and our loved ones. When we face denial, our ego may challenge us to take a step back and stop thinking of bending down again. We might have the patience to come again but we might not stay calm when we hear absurd & hurting words from the other side. We need to remind ourselves that rebuilding was our need and we have to bend down, again and again, to reconcile, to recreate and to rebuild.

6. Asking for Forgiveness:

We may say, "*I was not wrong*" when we are allowed to come close to the person with whom we want to restore our relationship. But we should remember that we were also part of that act of breaking our relationship. So, we need to ask forgiveness from our partner, our children, our parents or whoever it may be.

7. Having Faith in Our Love:

The Bible says '*love never fails.*' It is true. When we have true love springing up from our hearts nothing can stop us. Love never fails. So, we need to have faith in our love for our beloved. That will win the battle for us.

I have never mentioned that these are the 7 steps to reconcile and rebuild, rather I said that these are the 7 important factors involved in the process of reconciling and rebuilding. All these factors have to work together. It's not that we should finish the first step and then try out the second one. All these have to work together and only then can expect a rebuilt relationship.

Friends! Let's start our reconciling and rebuilding process with a word of prayer. May God bless us to cherish a reconciled and rebuilt relationship.

"***Bear with each other and forgive one another***
if any of you has a grievance against someone.
Forgive as the Lord forgave you."
Colossians 3:13

FIFTEEN

PICK YOUR TRUE IDENTITY

"Who exactly am I?"

Have you ever pondered that question? I asked myself that question a few years ago when I was struggling to find my life's purpose.

Let me explain the FOUR basic determinants of our identity. I abbreviate them P I C K to make them easier to remember (though the pointers are not according to the right order).

P – PURPOSE OF LIFE

Understanding your life's purpose reveals your true identity to both yourself and others. Allow me to explain what I just said so you can understand.

The web definition of 'Identity Crisis' is *"a period of uncertainty and confusion in which a person's sense of identity becomes insecure, typically due to a change in their expected aims or role in society."*

According to psychologist Erik Erikson, *"an identity crisis is a time of intensive analysis and exploration of different ways of looking at oneself."*

During the adolescent years, according to Erikson's stages of psychosocial development, people struggle between feelings of identity versus role confusion.

When a person knows and understands his or her life's purpose, he or she is clear on what to do and what not to do. People feel confident and at ease with what they do or decide to do next. During adolescence or the teenage years, he or she goes through difficult periods of defining his or her own role in society and dealing with the issue of an identity crisis.

We are all aware that the purpose of life motivates people. Our life's purpose drives us to pursue a particular career or profession in order to earn a living.

Through our profession, our purpose determines our identity. For example, our identity becomes 'A Teacher' when our purpose in life is to build the foundation of children through education.

I – IMAGE IN WHICH WE WERE CREATED

> *"So God created mankind in his own image,*
> *in the image of God He created them;*
> *male and female he created them."*

We need to understand that God, our creator, created us in His own image, which becomes our identity. Before we judge someone for being beautiful or ugly, we must recognise that we are rejecting God's image. Although sin and self-gratification have tarnished our original image or identity, yet we must always remember that we are all humans, men and women, created in the image of the Creator God.

C – CHARACTERISTICS WE POSSESS

Our identity is also determined by the characteristics we have and the characteristics we develop as we grow older. People identify or recognise us based on our characteristics, which are similar to our faces. For example, if I have the characteristic of helping and serving everyone around me, people will identify me as a helpful man. Similarly, when I lie to everyone in everything, people label me a liar.

K – KNOWLEDGE WE ACQUIRE

We gain knowledge as we grow in health and mind as a result of our education and interests. We discover our talents and hone them with the knowledge we've gained from various sources. And our knowledge gives us a sense of self and identity.

Children who excel in school are considered 'very intelligent.' We identify and label others as 'idiots or fools' in the same way.

If we arrange the pointers correctly, it could be "**I C P K**" because Image comes first, Characteristic comes second, Purpose comes third, and Knowledge comes last. But for the sake of simplicity, let's stick with ***PICK***.

Are you unsure of who you are?

Consider your life's purpose, acknowledge that you were created in the image of the Creator God, and understand that the characteristics you possess and the knowledge you acquire will make you known to those around you.

So, are you prepared to **P I C K** your Identity?

9 798889 862642

Printed by Libri Plureos GmbH in Hamburg,
Germany